BUILDING BY DESIGN

ENGINEERING THE GOLDEN GATE BRIDGE

BY KATE CONLEY

CONTENT CONSULTANT
Harvey Schwartz
Author, *Building the Golden Gate Bridge: A Workers' Oral History*

Cover image: The iconic Golden Gate Bridge stretches across San Francisco Bay in California.

Core Library
An Imprint of Abdo Publishing
abdopublishing.com

abdopublishing.com

Published by Abdo Publishing, a division of ABDO, PO Box 398166, Minneapolis, Minnesota 55439.

Printed in the United States of America, North Mankato, Minnesota
052017
092017

THIS BOOK CONTAINS RECYCLED MATERIALS

Cover Photo: Shutterstock Images
Interior Photos: Shutterstock Images, 1, 14, 36–37, 45; iStockphoto, 4–5, 12–13, 18, 43; AP Images, 7, 34; Red Line Editorial, 8; Bettmann/Getty Images, 10; Valerie Loiseleux/iStockphoto, 16; Underwood Archives/Archive Photos/Getty Images, 22–23, 29, 31; George Rinhart/Corbis Historical/Getty Images, 24; Fox Photos/Hulton Archive/Getty Images, 27; David Boyer/National Geographic/Getty Images, 38

Editor: Heidi Schoof
Imprint Designer: Maggie Villaume
Series Design Direction: Laura Polzin

Publisher's Cataloging-in-Publication Data

Names: Conley, Kate, author.
Title: Engineering the Golden Gate Bridge / by Kate Conley.
Description: Minneapolis, MN : Abdo Publishing, 2018. | Series: Building by design | Includes bibliographical references and index.
Identifiers: LCCN 2017930241 | ISBN 9781532111662 (lib. bdg.) | ISBN 9781680789515 (ebook)
Subjects: LCSH: Structural engineering--Miscellanea--Juvenile literature. | Golden Gate Bridge (San Francisco, Calif.)--Design and construction--Juvenile literature. | Civil engineering--Juvenile literature. | Buildings, structures, etc.--Juvenile literature.
Classification: DDC 624--dc23
LC record available at http://lccn.loc.gov/2017930241

CONTENTS

CHAPTER ONE

ACROSS THE GOLDEN GATE

On many summer days in San Francisco, California, a thick fog blankets the bay. Two orange towers rise above the fog like ladders leading to the sky. They are the only clues to the marvel of engineering hidden in the fog below. The towers anchor the city's Golden Gate Bridge.

Since the bridge opened in 1937, more than 2 billion cars have driven across it. But the bridge is more than just a way to get

Morning and evening fog from the Pacific Ocean rolls into San Francisco Bay through the Golden Gate most days from June to August.

across the Golden Gate Strait. Its graceful lines, bright orange color, and beautiful setting make it a work of art. Its distinct profile has become a symbol of the United States. It is also a feat of modern engineering.

SUSPENSION BRIDGES

The Golden Gate Bridge is a suspension bridge. This type of bridge uses towers at each end. The bridge deck is suspended from cables attached to the towers. The deck has no supports underneath it, as many other types of bridges do. Suspension bridges are most useful over large spans.

THE BRIDGE THAT COULDN'T BE BUILT

The quest to build the bridge began in an unlikely way. It started when a powerful earthquake shook San Francisco on April 18, 1906. The earthquake lasted less than one minute. As the ground shook, candles and gas lamps tipped over. They ignited fires that burned across the city for three days. More than 28,000 buildings were destroyed.

The San Francisco earthquake of 1906 broke open gas and water mains, leaving no way to stop fires from destroying nearly 500 city blocks.

The city lay in ruins. Its residents needed new homes, offices, and public buildings. The city also needed new roads and bridges. Mayor James Rolph appointed a city engineer to oversee this work. His name was Michael O'Shaughnessy. As part of the rebuilding effort, O'Shaughnessy dreamed of building a bridge across the Golden Gate Strait.

For years, nothing happened. The project was too difficult. A bridge across the strait would need to be nearly two miles (3 km) long. No one had ever made a suspension bridge that long before. The bridge would also need to be incredibly strong. It would have to

THE GOLDEN GATE BRIDGE

The Golden Gate Strait is the natural entrance to San Francisco Bay. This map shows how the Golden Gate Bridge connects San Francisco with Marin County over the strait. Is it different from the way you imagined it after reading Chapter One? How does seeing the map help you better understand the need for a bridge across the Golden Gate Strait?

withstand earthquakes, high winds, and strong currents. Many people criticized the project. They said a bridge like that couldn't be built.

JOSEPH B. STRAUSS

The bridge project did not move forward, but the city's other rebuilding went well. San Francisco grew quickly.

But the city's growth was limited by its border on the bay. The only way to get across San Francisco Bay was by ferry. Cars waiting in line for the ferry created terrible traffic jams in the city. The interest in building a bridge grew.

DON'T BUILD THE BRIDGE!

The Golden Gate Bridge did not please everyone. The Southern Pacific ferry service strongly opposed it. Every weekday, it ferried 50,000 workers across the bay. With a bridge they could drive across the bay themselves. The US War Department also opposed the bridge. It feared the bridge would be an easy target for an enemy to destroy. Doing so would potentially block the harbor and trap ships inside it.

O'Shaughnessy wanted to find an experienced engineer for the project. In 1919 he contacted Joseph B. Strauss. Strauss had designed nearly 400 bridges. He agreed to design a bridge across the bay.

Strauss worked for more than a year on the design. In 1921 he presented his plans. City officials and the

Joseph B. Strauss built a team of experts and was the leading force behind the design and construction of the Golden Gate Bridge.

public disliked it from the start. It was clunky and ugly. Critics compared it to an upside-down rat trap. San Francisco and the cities north of the bay disagreed on how to move forward. The long-awaited bridge project was once again at a standstill.

A NEW DESIGN

In December 1928, the cities found a way to work together. They created the Golden Gate Bridge and Highway District. It appointed Strauss as the chief engineer. By this time, Strauss agreed that his original plan should be scrapped. Consulting engineers suggested a more graceful bridge design. Two tall towers held long, swooping cables that supported a suspended bridge deck. Design engineer Charles Ellis used math to consider the forces at work on such a bridge. Ellis performed thousands of calculations to complete the design.

The new bridge design was better looking. But crews would have to climb to dizzying heights to install the towers and cables. Divers would face dangers as they worked deep underwater building the foundation. The cost to build the bridge would be staggering. Even if all the obstacles could be overcome, no one knew if the bridge would be safe and sturdy. It would require courage, determination, and a leap of faith.

FURTHER EVIDENCE

Chapter One mentions how the Golden Gate Bridge is considered not just a bridge, but an amazing work of art. Read the article at the website below. What other information can you find about the idea that the bridge is a work of art?

MONUMENT, WORK OF ART, STAR

abdocorelibrary.com/engineering-the-golden-gate-bridge

CHAPTER TWO

DESIGNING A LANDMARK

The soaring orange towers and graceful cables have made the Golden Gate Bridge a landmark. But it is also a complex structure that thousands of people rely on every day. Each part of the bridge was engineered to survive a variety of situations safely. The bridge handles heavy traffic, high winds, and even earthquakes with ease.

Engineers call the parts of the bridge above the water the superstructure. It gives the bridge its shape and design. The parts hidden below the water are called the substructure. They anchor the bridge and give it support.

The north tower of the Golden Gate Bridge rises tall above the scenic highlands of Marin County.

PARTS OF A SUSPENSION BRIDGE

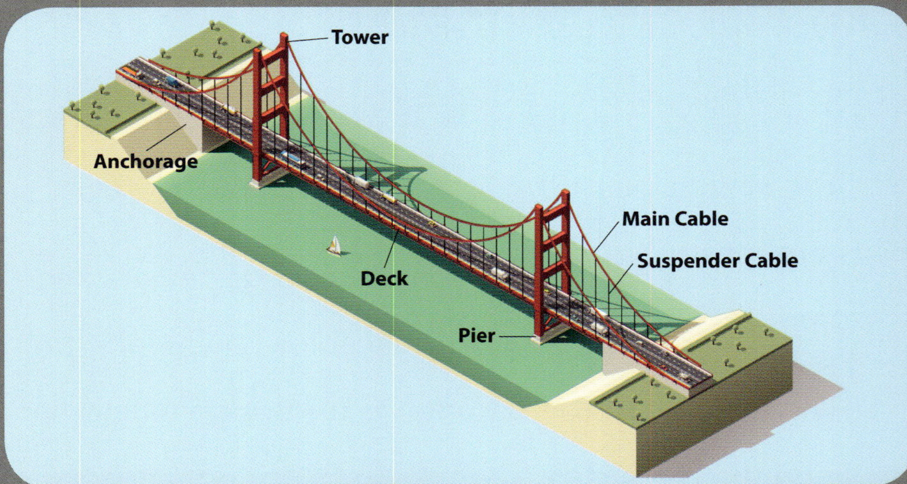

A suspension bridge requires several elements to work in harmony. Each element has a different job. If one element fails, the bridge will not be safe. Anchors secure cables, which carry the load from the deck. Each tower provides tension on the cables to keep the deck suspended. The tension creates a downward force on the towers that is absorbed by the piers. How does seeing all the parts together in the finished bridge help you understand how these elements work in harmony?

All parts of a suspension bridge must work in harmony to keep the bridge steady and safe.

TOWERS AND PIERS

The bridge towers are part of the superstructure. One stands on each end of the bay. Their job is to hold the bridge's cables in place. The weight of the cables and the deck rests on the two slender towers. It creates a strong downward pressure called compression.

The towers resist this incredible force using piers. Piers are massive concrete pillars with steel bars inside for strength. The towers sit on top of the piers.

The downward force from the towers presses down on the piers. The piers rest on bedrock under the ocean floor. The bedrock absorbs all the force of the compression from the towers. This keeps the towers upright and the bridge safe.

CABLES AND TENSION

The cables are another part of the superstructure. The Golden Gate Bridge has two main cables. They hang between the towers and form the bridge's gentle U-shaped curves. The cables carry the weight of the bridge deck to the two towers. They are made of thousands of thin steel wires bound together.

A cross-section displayed in Strauss Plaza demonstrates how each main cable is made up of 27,572 individual steel wires.

Steel suspender ropes hang down from the main cables. The suspender ropes connect the main cables and the bridge deck. The deck is heavy, and gravity pulls it down. The downward pull causes the cables to stretch. That stretching is a force called tension.

The tension on the cables must be offset, or the bridge will collapse. Engineers used anchorages for this job. Anchorages hold the main cables tight. The cables end in an anchorage on both sides of the bridge. The anchorages are connected to bedrock with steel plates, rods, and eye bars.

Each anchorage has 61 eye bars. These are metal rods with holes at the tips. The hole in each eye bar pokes out of the surface of the concrete. The wires of the main cables are fastened to the holes in the eye bars. This system keeps the cables from sagging under the weight of the bridge deck.

DO THE MATH

The Golden Gate Bridge was designed entirely by hand. Engineers did not have computers or calculators. Charles Ellis was an engineer and an expert mathematician. He was responsible for testing the bridge's design through mathematics to see if it would work. If he made mistakes, the bridge could fail. Using only a slide rule, pencil, and paper, Ellis spent 20 months working out all the mathematical calculations needed for the bridge design.

LIVE AND DEAD LOADS

When designing the Golden Gate Bridge, engineers paid close attention to load. This is the weight a bridge must support. The cars, trucks, and people that cross a bridge are called the live load. Engineers estimate how

The length of each pair of steel suspender ropes is carefully calculated to evenly distribute the load of the bridge deck.

much live load can safely cross the bridge. The live load changes depending on the traffic levels.

As the load increases, so does the tension on the cables. Increased tension lowers the deck. The change in the deck's position is called deflection. The cables on the Golden Gate Bridge allow for deflection by stretching. A heavy live load can pull the bridge deck 10.8 feet (3.3 m) lower than normal without safety problems.

The weight of the bridge itself is also part of its load. This is called the dead load. To offset it, engineers needed to find building materials that were light but strong. Their solution was metal cables. The cables are much lighter than the metal beams used in other types of bridges.

EFFECTS OF THE WIND

Wind causes additional load on a bridge. When wind blows from side to side across the bridge, it is called a static wind load. To prevent wind from knocking down the deck, engineers designed the Golden Gate Bridge to have flexibility. As winds

GALLOPING GERTIE

On July 1, 1940, the Tacoma Narrows Bridge opened. The suspension bridge spanned Puget Sound in the state of Washington. It did not take long for people to worry about the bridge's safety. When winds blew, the bridge deck rippled noticeably. People nicknamed the bridge "Galloping Gertie."

On November 7, 1940, a strong wind made Galloping Gertie's deck ripple wildly. Soon the deck began to twist violently from side to side. Highway officials closed the bridge. Then a large section of the deck broke free, and the bridge collapsed. The bridge had failed because its deck was not stiff enough. It could not absorb the load from the strong winds.

blow, the cables allow the bridge to swing. It can move 27.7 feet (8.4 m) from side to side and remain safe.

When wind blows up and down on a bridge, it is called a dynamic wind load. It can make the bridge's deck twist and buckle. Sometimes the movement can be violent enough to shake apart the bridge. To prevent this, engineers used trusses in the Golden Gate's deck. The trusses make the deck stiff. A stiff deck moves less in a dynamic wind load.

Another way engineers solved the problem of wind load was in the tower design. The towers have several openings in them. They allow the wind to pass through the towers without meeting resistance.

Every element of the bridge design was carefully planned. Ellis and the other engineers worked tirelessly to design a bridge that would be safe and stable. But turning the plans into reality would be an even greater challenge.

STRAIGHT TO THE SOURCE

Charles Ellis was confident in the ability of the structure to stand up to the region's earthquakes. He compared it to waiting out the quake in the safety of centuries-old redwood trees:

> *If I knew that there was to be an earthquake in San Francisco tomorrow and I couldn't get into an airplane and had to remain in the city, I think I should get a piece of clothesline about 1,000 or 2,000 feet long, and a hammock, and I would string it from the tops of two of the tallest redwoods I could find, get into the hammock and feel reasonably safe. If this bridge were built at that time, I would [go quickly] to the center of it, and while watching the sun sink into China across the Pacific, I would feel content with the thought that in case of an earthquake, I had chosen the safest spot in which to be.*

Source: John Van der Zee. *The Gate: The True Story of the Design and Construction of the Golden Gate Bridge*. New York: Simon and Schuster, 1986. Print. 101.

What's the Big Idea?

What is the connection between Ellis's image of a hammock strung from redwoods and the Golden Gate Bridge? What do the two images have in common? Why would either of these settings protect a person during an earthquake?

CHAPTER
THREE

BUILDING THE GOLDEN GATE BRIDGE

On February 26, 1933, more than 100,000 people flocked to Crissy Field. This military airfield was located on San Francisco Bay, near the site of the proposed bridge. The crowds had come to celebrate the official groundbreaking for the Golden Gate Bridge.

ANCHORING THE BRIDGE

Crews began the project by building the bridge's anchorages. Each one was made of three interlocking concrete blocks. It was a

Fort Point, a brick fortress, was originally going to be demolished for bridge construction. Instead, engineers designed the bridge to go over the fort.

The massive cable anchorages at each end of the Golden Gate Bridge were specially designed to withstand the Bay Area's frequent earthquakes.

special design made for the site. Since the area sits close to the San Andreas fault line, earthquakes are common. This interlocking block design would prevent the anchorages from slipping during an earthquake.

Crews built a wooden mold for the base block and filled it with concrete. The next layer was the anchor block. Crews installed steel girders to strengthen the block. They also added the eye bars. This entire layer was then covered in more concrete. Finally, crews built the weight block. Its massive quantities of concrete would hold the lower two blocks in place. When the anchors were completed, only the openings for the eye bars were visible above the blocks.

THE NORTH PIER

Before crews could begin building the piers, they had to make a dry workspace for themselves in the bay. This space is called a cofferdam. To create it, a barge brought in a tall metal frame filled with crushed rock. Workers sunk it above the site where the pier would sit.

Next, workers placed sheet metal around the frame. They sealed the joints to make them watertight. Then they used powerful pumps to remove all the water from inside the frame. The sheet metal kept any new water from getting in. Now workers had a dry space to begin their work.

To build the north pier, workers used powerful drills and dynamite to clear the soil in the cofferdam. They had to go down 33 feet (10 m) before they reached bedrock. With the base for the pier dug, they began to pour concrete. For days, crews worked around the clock

A DANGEROUS JOB

Working on the Golden Gate Bridge was a dangerous job. Strauss had strict safety rules. Workers were required to wear hardhats. Anyone caught acting recklessly was automatically fired. A safety net, set up in 1936, spanned the underside of the bridge to catch any workers who fell. An on-site hospital treated injuries quickly. The safety measures were mostly effective. Up until 1937, only one person had died while working on the bridge. Then on February 17, 1937, a scaffold fell and tore the safety net. Ten workers who had been on the scaffold died.

to pour concrete. When it was completed, the pier reached 44 feet (13 m) above the water line of the bay.

THE SOUTH PIER

Building the south pier was more difficult. It jutted 1,125 feet (343 m) off shore. It was the first time anyone had attempted to build a bridge support in deep, open water. Work started with the construction of a fender. It was like an oval-shaped fence. The fender would protect the tower from any ships in the bay that might hit it accidentally during foggy weather.

Divers performed dangerous work deep underwater to construct the fender and pier for the south tower.

To build the fender, divers placed dynamite in the floor of the bay. They needed to blast through it to reach bedrock. Divers then used high-pressure hoses to clear materials loosened by the dynamite. When the bedrock was finally reached, divers put funnels and watertight molds into place underwater. Then crews could begin to pour concrete into them to form the fender.

With the fender complete, crews pumped the water out of it. A dry area the size of a football field remained. Workers dug 110 feet (34 m) below sea level to reach bedrock. Then they began pouring the concrete for the south pier until it rose 44 feet (13 m) above the bay's surface. When the concrete dried, workers refilled the area between the fender and the pier with water.

RAISING THE TOWERS

With the piers in place, construction could begin on the towers. Workers built the towers from steel. Their job was to rivet together the steel pieces of the tower. They worked from scaffolds to reach the growing towers easily. Each tower is made of two legs that are 90 feet (27 m) apart. Metal beams called struts and crossbars join the legs together.

The completed towers are a sight to behold. They rise 746 feet (227 m) above the bay. They were the world's tallest bridge towers at the time of their construction. The parts of the towers that can be seen

Riveters work in cages on the south tower. The rivets create patterns that add to the unique design of the bridge.

above the road received special artistic treatment. Architect Irving Morrow created Art Deco details, such as fluting that runs up and down the sides of the towers. It creates a feeling of movement as the sun shines on them. Morrow's additions have led many people to see the bridge as a piece of art.

Morrow also chose the color for the towers. He settled on a color called international orange. It blends in with the hills nearby and contrasts with the blue of the bay and the sky. The orange color also makes the towers visible in the thick fog that commonly covers the bay.

SPINNING THE CABLES

By mid-1935, the towers were ready to support the two massive main cables. The cables were so large and heavy, they had to be made on site. To do this, workers attached a steel wire as thin as a pencil to an eye bar on one anchor. They used a spinning wheel to carry the wire over both towers and down to the eye bar on the opposite shore.

Spinning the cables was a slow process. It had to be repeated until each main cable was just over three feet (1 m) in diameter and 7,650 feet (2,332 m) long. Gradually, workers figured out how to speed up the process. They color coded the wires and used

As the cable was spun, workers on the catwalk bundled the wires and placed them in cable formers.

six spinning wheels at once. On an eight-hour shift, they could spin 1,000 miles (1,600 km) of wire. The cables were completed in slightly more than six months.

Workers installed grooved metal bands along the length of the main cables. Five hundred suspender ropes were placed in those grooves. They connect the two main cables with the bridge deck. The suspender ropes are spaced 50 feet (15 m) apart from each other. They vary in length. Those near the center of the bridge are less than 10 feet (3 m) long. Those closest to the towers hang down nearly 500 feet (152 m).

HANGING THE DECK

The next step was hanging the bridge deck. To do this, crews bolted pairs of suspender ropes together. This created a cradle on which the deck would sit. The deck was made of steel beams supported by trusses. Workers installed the deck in 747 sections. To spread the heavy load, crews began from each tower and worked toward the center.

With the deck in place, crews could pave the roadway. They completed their work on April 19, 1937. Four days later, bridge workers held a special ceremony. Ironworker Edward "Iron Horse" Stanley tried to install a gold rivet on the bridge to mark its completion.

The gold was much softer than the steel used in the regular rivets. It crumbled when Stanley pounded it in. Workers hammered in a regular steel rivet, and the bridge was finally complete.

WORKING ON THE BRIDGE

From the start, Strauss and his team of engineers knew they were undertaking a special project. It did not take the workers long to realize this either. Harold McClain, one of the workers, recalled this feeling with fondness: "You couldn't help know it. You were building the greatest structure in the world. You knew one thing for sure—there wasn't going to be anything else like it."

In May the public had the opportunity to celebrate the bridge's completion at the Opening Fiesta Week. Local schools and businesses closed so everyone could join the fun. May 27 was the first day of the celebration. That day the bridge was open to pedestrians only from dawn to dusk. People could pay 25 cents to walk across it. Throughout the day, 200,000 people walked, ran, roller skated, and

Five hundred planes from US Navy aircraft carriers took part in the opening festivities on May 28, 1937.

even tap danced their way across the Golden Gate. The bridge that critics said couldn't be built stood tall in the bay at last, a marvel of engineering and art.

STRAIGHT TO THE SOURCE

When the Golden Gate Bridge was completed, Strauss wrote a poem in its honor. It expresses the scale and strength of the bridge he helped create:

At last the mighty task is done;
Resplendent in the western sun
The Bridge looms mountain high;
Its titan piers grip ocean floor,
Its great steel arms link shore with shore,
Its towers pierce the sky.

On its broad decks in rightful pride,
The world in swift parade shall ride,
Throughout all time to be
Beneath, fleet ships from every port,
Vast landlocked bay, historic fort,
And dwarfing all—the sea.

Source: "Strauss Poems." *Golden Gate Bridge.* GoldenGateBridge.org, 2017. Web. Accessed February 23, 2017.

Point of View

How does Strauss describe the bridge? What does his description say about his point of view on the structure?

CHAPTER FOUR

THE GOLDEN GATE BRIDGE TODAY

When the idea for a bridge across San Francisco Bay first arose, people said it was impossible. Strauss and his team of engineers and architects pushed the limits of math and science to make the bridge a reality. Their bridge seamlessly blended science and art in a way that is rarely done.

MAINTENANCE

In the years since it opened, the bridge has performed well. It has withstood earthquakes,

The Golden Gate Bridge is an essential part of the American landscape and an amazing engineering triumph.

For decades, painters have helped protect the bridge's outer surface.

windstorms, and heavy traffic. The Golden Gate Bridge, Highway, and Transportation District maintains the bridge. Its biggest job is keeping the bridge painted so the metal parts don't rust. A crew of painters works throughout the year to keep the bridge's paint fresh.

Other maintenance workers inspect the bridge every day. They make sure no bolts are loose. They check the steel for signs of cracks or weaknesses. The cables are also inspected to make sure they show no signs of fraying or stress. This constant attention to the bridge's maintenance has kept it in good shape for many decades.

USING THE BRIDGE

Every day, approximately 112,000 cars cross the Golden Gate Bridge. This volume of cars has the potential to create large traffic jams. The Golden Gate Bridge has systems to stop this from happening too often. It uses reversible lanes and one-way tolls to keep traffic moving.

Reversible lanes allow the bridge to adjust to current traffic levels. The bridge has six lanes. The medians that separate the lanes can be moved. Special vehicles called zipper trucks do this work. They ride on top of the medians and shift them into a new position.

RUST

Water, salt, and steel are a recipe for corrosion. Corrosion is a chemical reaction. It causes a reddish-brown layer called rust to form on metal. Rust weakens steel. It can cause cracks and holes in the metal. Fighting rust is a constant battle on the Golden Gate Bridge. Covering the bridge's steel with a coat of paint protects it from the bay's damp, salty air. This slows rust and keeps the bridge strong.

Drivers on the Golden Gate Bridge must pay a toll to use it. The money collected from the tolls pays for the bridge's maintenance. It also helps pay for bus and ferry transportation. Drivers pay a toll only when they head south, into San Francisco.

SETTING RECORDS

For nearly 30 years, the Golden Gate Bridge was the world's longest suspension bridge. Never before could people bridge such a distance. Today, Japan, China, Denmark, and England have suspension bridges longer than the Golden Gate. But none of them would have been possible without the daring and skill required to build the Golden Gate.

Drivers are not the only people who use the bridge. Walkers and bikers often travel across the bridge to enjoy the beautiful views of the bay. Each end of the bridge is also part of the Golden Gate National Recreation Area. It is one of the world's largest national parks in a city setting. It provides access to beaches, historic buildings, and overlooks.

THE GOLDEN GATE'S LEGACY

The original purpose of the Golden Gate Bridge was to connect San Francisco with several counties to the north. The bridge allowed communities on either side of it to grow and prosper.

But it ended up being much more than just a bridge. It became a national landmark as recognizable as the Statue of Liberty or Mount Rushmore. It became an example of how a functional structure could also be a stunning piece of art. It is a symbol of human achievement.

EXPLORE ONLINE

Chapter Four describes how one of the key maintenance tasks on the bridge is keeping it painted to avoid rust. The article at the website below includes more information on how the painting process works. What new details can you learn from this article about how and why the Golden Gate Bridge is painted?

PAINTING THE GOLDEN GATE BRIDGE

abdocorelibrary.com/engineering-the-golden-gate-bridge

FAST FACTS

- The Golden Gate Bridge spans the Golden Gate Strait in San Francisco, California.
- Joseph Strauss made the bridge's original design and was the project's biggest champion.
- Engineer Charles Ellis completed the final design using complicated mathematical equations.
- At the time it was built, the Golden Gate Bridge was the world's longest suspension bridge.
- The span of the Golden Gate Bridge is 4,200 feet (1,280 m) long.
- Engineers had to consider the live load, dead load, and wind load when designing the bridge.
- The Golden Gate's cables allow the bridge to move safely with the wind, earthquakes, or heavy traffic loads.
- Architect Irving Morrow chose the orange color of the towers to stand out in the fog but also blend in with the surrounding mountains.
- The Golden Gate Bridge opened to the public on May 27, 1937.
- The bay's damp, salty air makes rust a problem in maintaining the bridge.

- The bridge has reversible lanes and one-way tolls to reduce traffic jams.
- More than 2 billion cars have traveled across the bridge since it opened.

STOP AND THINK

Say What?

Studying engineering can mean learning a lot of new vocabulary. Make a list of five engineering terms in this book that you'd never heard before. Use a dictionary to find out what they mean. Then write the meanings in your own words and use each term in a new sentence.

Surprise Me

Chapter Two discusses the science behind suspension bridges. What surprised you most about how they work? Choose three facts about suspension bridges that surprised you. Why did they surprise you?

Tell the Tale

The end of Chapter Three describes the bridge's official opening in May 1937. Imagine you are one of the 200,000 people who walked across the bridge that day. Write a paragraph describing what you see, hear, and smell as you cross the bridge. Why do you choose to attend the grand opening?

Dig Deeper

After reading this book, what questions do you still have about the Golden Gate Bridge? With an adult's help, find a few reliable sources that can help you answer your questions. Write a paragraph about what you learned.

GLOSSARY

Art Deco
a style of art and design that began in the 1920s and used geometric shapes, sleek lines, and bold colors

bedrock
solid rock that lies under the surface of the ground or seafloor

fluting
decorative grooves on a column

girder
a large metal beam

interlocking
fitting together by overlapping

median
a barrier between opposing lanes of traffic

rivet
a metal pin that joins two metal plates

scaffold
a moveable platform for working high above the ground

slide rule
a ruler with a variety of scales printed on it and a slider that moves across them, allowing the user to calculate complex mathematical equations

truss
a frame of beams that supports a bridge

LEARN MORE

Books

Farndon, John. *Engineers*. New York: DK Publishing, 2015.

Finger, Brad. *13 Bridges Children Should Know.* New York: Prestel, 2015.

Latham, Donna. *Bridges and Tunnels: Investigate Feats of Engineering.* White River Junction, VT: Nomad Press, 2012.

Websites

To learn more about Building by Design, visit **abdobooklinks.com**. These links are routinely monitored and updated to provide the most current information available.

Visit **abdocorelibrary.com** for free additional tools for teachers and students.

INDEX

About the Author

Kate Conley has been writing nonfiction books for children for nearly two decades. When she's not writing, Conley spends her time reading, sewing, and solving crossword puzzles. She lives in Minnesota with her husband and two children.